THROUGH IT ALL
The Lord Sustained Me

Copyright © 2019 Patricia Obichukwu.
All rights reserved. First paperback edition printed 2019 in the United Kingdom
a catalogue record for this book is available
from the British Library.
ISBN 978-1-913455-00-2
No part of this book shall be reproduced or transmitted in any form or by any means, electronic or mechanical, including photocopying, recording, or by any information retrieval system without written permission of the publisher.
Published by Scribblecity Publications.
Printed in Great Britain
Although every precaution has been taken in
the preparation of this book, the publisher and author assume no responsibility for errors or omissions. Neither is any liability assumed for damages resulting from the use of this information contained herein.

Acknowledgements

Firstly, my special appreciation and thanksgiving goes to my Heavenly Father, the King of Kings and the Lord of Lords, My Lord and saviour Jesus Christ for all He has done in making this book a reality. To God alone be all the glory, honour and praise for His faithfulness and grace.

I want to give special thanks to my dearest sister and friend Ms Mary Nkafu for using her excellent skills and knowledge to make this book come to life by typing the original transcript. My gratitude also goes to my darling sisters and friends Dr CarolyneTah and Ligia Mladenova for their reviews in shaping the final content of this book.

My special thanks and appreciation goes to my darling brother, friend and mentor Dr Tony Peters, a well-seasoned man of God, for your time in writing the forward for this book. I will like to sincerely appreciate Barbara Ifezue and her team for all the hard work in producing the final piece of this book.

As you read this book and go through the journey with Precious, may you be enriched with wisdom and understanding to help you find hope and victory which comes only by trusting in the Lord Jesus Christ the maker of all things.

Be encouraged and know that you are not alone.

Patricia Obichukwu (PNO)

Dedication

This book is dedicated to my precious children – Wendy, Emma, Michael & Daniel, and my grandchildren – Benjamin, Naomi and Isaiah.

In memory of my late husband Nkem Godwin and many women who have experienced life challenging circumstances in their relationships and may be at a place of giving up.
This book will encourage them to hold on to Jesus as the source of hope.

Based on a true life story of a woman who had gone through the rough challenges of life and was able to stir through the storms trusting in God Almighty who brought her out of it all successfully to the glory of His mighty name.

From being rejected as a child by her father to having an unstable marriage relationship, her faith in Jesus stirred her through all life's storms to restoration, restitution, replenishment and replication.

Foreword

Life can often appear to be confusing and brutal; but only if you observe it with a fatalistic disposition or mindset. The truth is that life is not as random and as unplanned as it sometimes appears to be. When you are holding unto God's Sovereign hand, your life (and everything you experience) always has a point to it. It has a purpose and it has a reason.

God once explained it this way to one of His Servants. He said: "I know the thoughts that I am thinking towards you—they are thoughts of peace and not of evil, to give you a great future and a lasting hope." In other words, "God was saying, just because life is shaky or uncertain does not mean it is aimless or unguided—because I have a great plan."

"Through it all" is a story of one woman's epic battle to stay afloat in an ocean of challenges, trials and pain. The ups and downs of life can dazzle anyone, but when they are inflicted on you by your family, they become larger than life. They overwhelm you and turn your world up-side-down.

Such was the situation in the life of Precious.

But Precious had something. She had a secret weapon. And all she had to do was learn how to use it. She had to learn how to deflect the trauma and accusations of her enemies. She had to learn how to steady her nerves; how to pull on her Source of power; and how to (not just survive) but thrive. It wasn't easy, but through it all, she did it.

As you read through the pages of this book, you too may come to discover your secret weapon. You may find that everything you've had to go through (and everything you are still going through) is designed to make you a winner at life. If so, the time you spend reading this book would be a profitable investment. So, learn as many lessons as you can from "Through it all" — then pass it on!

Tony Peters
Senior Minister
The King's House
(London's Alive Church)

Table of Contents

Foreword	*vi*
Introduction	*1*
Formative Years	*4*
The Nigerian Civil War	*8*
Rebuilding After the Civil War	*16*
Teenage Life Experience	*22*
Marriage Proposal	*29*
Life Overseas	*38*
The Honeymoon Adventure	*46*
Life in the UK	*50*
The Gathering Storm	*56*
Searching for God	*61*
The Breaking Storm	*70*
Beyond Cultural and Traditional Norms	*82*
Through it All	*88*
Epilogue	*105*

CHAPTER 1
INTRODUCTION

Petite and light in complexion, her slender frame and long limbs gained her the nickname "Lanky." Precious was a perky young girl with a contagious smile. Her bubbly personality endeared her to those around her. Despite her lanky frame, Precious was agile on her feet and would sway her body gracefully to the dance of "The Young Maidens" that made her the envy of the community.

In those days, when more female children than male were born to a family, it was usually the parents' priority to educate the male child, and often the girls would be educated only to primary school level if they were lucky, and no further. With six girls and a boy in the family, Precious and her sisters experienced this "tradition." It didn't matter that she was extremely smart and articulate.

Introduction

Okoro Nnadi was a civil servant who worked with the East Central State Waterworks Board. Precious' grandfather on her maternal side had worked in the state courts. It was prestigious to work in the civil service back then, and there was deep respect for those who mingled with the "White Men," the Europeans who headed the companies. The Waterworks Board where Precious' father worked was located in Enugu, the capital city of the East Central State. It was 68 miles from their village, Ogidi, in the south eastern state of Nigeria, and because of the long commute, he would usually remain in his station for three months in a row.

In his absence, Precious' mum would hold the forte. Though a small woman, Mama Precious had a staggering strength and resourcefulness that enabled her to run her household efficiently. She was witty, spoke her mind freely, and was greatly admired by the villagers who would always come seeking one advice or another. In her forthright way, she would always say it as it was without mincing words. "Truthful Mama," she was fondly called. She was indeed a woman of integrity.

Each day, she would carry her white enamel basin with her hoe and cutlass and set off for the acre of choice farmland that lay behind Okoro Nnadi's compound. Her green fingers served her well as her farm produced bumper crops of vegetables, corn, cassava and cocoyam all year round. This was enough for the feeding of her large family, and she would often carry the rest to the local Eke market. Her customers flocked to her store looking for the fresh produce.

CHAPTER 2
FORMATIVE YEARS

Intelligent and articulate, Precious was a star pupil. Her bubbly personality made her teachers and the entire community love her, and they called her "Nwa oma" or good child. She always had a smile and a hug for everyone.

Unfortunately, her bubbly nature was shadowed whenever her father returned from work in Enugu. Precious would withdraw into herself. Her father's obvious display of preferential affection toward Ndidi, her younger sister, always filled her with sadness. He was stern with her, while letting Ndidi get away with everything. He paid Precious little or no attention and would never compliment her for her good school results, unlike Ndidi who he would shower with praise and gifts. In return she would milk the moment by reporting trivial things Precious has done. Precious watched from a distance, with a deep feeling of rejection, and a longing for her father to love her too. She couldn't comprehend such dislike.

Looking at the skinny young girl sitting in the corner from the side of his eyes, Okoro Nnadi muffled a growl. Where did this one come from? He wondered. He couldn't accept her. After all, why should he? It was an abomination. She wasn't his. The stories must be true. She bore no resemblance to the Okoro Nnadi family. Their ebony complexion and big boned build had always been their trademark for many generations. This one looked sickly with the complexion of a ripe mango. It had been whispered, that she was conceived through an amorous relationship between Mama Precious and that charlatan, Nebo, the farmer.

Though Precious looked very much like her mother, Okoro Nnadi wasn't convinced, and was more welcoming to Ndidi who took after his complexion and his stocky build.

This feeling of rejection hung over Precious like a

dark cloud. Sadly, she was always happy to see her father return to his place of work. Her joy was that she was loved by her community, and everyone welcomed her with open arms. The attention she received, unfortunately created a lot of animosity between her and her nemesis, Edna, who was jealous that Precious was always called to lead the local dance. Although they were age mates, Edna was stocky and much bigger than Precious. She was also less bright academically which earned her the name 'Thick head' or 'block head'.

She would always pick on Precious, and seemed to take pleasure in tormenting the young girl. She would deliberately seek her out just to throw tirades of abuse at her. Precious wondered what wrong she had done to Edna that made her so bitter and mean towards her. Anywhere she caught sight of Edna she would quickly scurry in the opposite direction. "Precious, what is it with you and this girl?" Her mother would query.
"Mama, I didn't do anything to her o," she would burst out almost in tears.
Mama's voice would then soften, "Don't mind her,

She is a jealous big for nothing troublemaker."

CHAPTER 3
THE NIGERIAN CIVIL WAR

It was July 1967. Okoro Nnadi was relieved to find he had arrived to his village in Ogidi. It was a whole day's journey pedalling from Enugu. He could still remember the panic that broke out when the controller announced that war had begun and everyone should go home. The roads were congested. There was a mad rush as people scrambled to get away from the East Central State capital and return to their different villages. After waiting hours for a bus back to Ogidi, Okoro Nnadi decided to cycle. He knew it was going to be quite a journey, as he had never ridden his bicycle for that distance, but this was "Oso Ndu" as it is called in Igbo language - a race for life.

The past months had ushered in an exodus of Igbos who were living in northern Nigeria fleeing to their home towns in south eastern Nigeria. Returnees reported that they were being killed indiscriminately up north. It was a time of uncertainty and fear as rumours of war and secession spread.

Precious was surprised to see her father flustered, pedalling into the compound, his portmanteau and bag securely tied to the back of the bicycle. "Mama Precious!" He called. There was panic in the strained voice that made Mama come running from the back yard. She put her hands on her head, letting out a cry as he broke the news.

Her father and his brothers gathered their households, and it was agreed that Uncle Chudi's tipper lorry would transport the women and children to one of their in-laws' compound in Nnobi, which was further away and distant from the major roads.

A few months later, Precious and her family returned to their village in Ogidi, and on returning, they found that all the young men, including her only brother and cousins, had been drafted into the army. It was a solemn time, not knowing if they would ever see them again.

Although, they had returned to their homes, there was still a general unease, as the war was not yet over, and enemy forces were still advancing. There were times Precious saw truckloads of Biafran soldiers drive past the village. The ominous presence of war hung heavily in the air.

One day Precious went to visit her aunt, Philo, who lived along the major Enugu - Onitsha road that led to the capital city, Enugu, and other neigbouring towns. All of a sudden, there were sounds of bullets raining down around the house. In an instant, her aunt hurriedly grabbed her by the arm as well as whatever else she could lay hands on, and they began to run toward Precious' family house which was further in, away from the major road. Every now and then they would hide behind trees to dodge the raging bullets. Even when they could no longer hear the shelling, they ran non-stop until they got to the Okoro Nnadi's compound where they were ushered into a bunker. That night, they all slept inside the bunker hiding from the heavy military bombardment which was slowly encroaching upon their village.

Early in the morning, before cockcrow, the entire family gathered their few belongings and once again fled to Umuoji, a neighbouring town two villages away and a peaceful haven for some of the refugees from Ogidi.

In Umuoji town, they could see the war planes roar loudly past in the sky; the ground would tremble as bombs were dropped, sending people scurrying for cover. Sadly, many people were killed in the markets and neigbouring villages.

It was a frightening experience and a time of uncertainty for Precious and her family. Now and then her older sisters would go to their village, Ogidi, to get some food like plantains and yams from the farms around their homestead.

The Biafran army had occupied their village, and were using it as a station, while the Nigerian army had taken over her Aunty Philo's village which was located near the major road to Enugu. The soldiers in Precious' father's house were not pleasant. There was a day she accompanied her sisters to get some food, and they seized her and her two sisters and locked them in the bunker while they took the eldest one to their senior officer. It was several hours before they released them. They threatened to kill them if they ever returned.

With no means of gaining access to their farmlands, hunger and malnutrition had begun to rummage their lives. The war had divided the eastern state into two, with the Biafran soldiers on one side and the Nigerian soldiers on the other.

One day, Precious' elder sisters decided to take a dangerous trip to a town called Otuocha, situated far from Enugu-Onitsha main road. There, the indigenes were still able to farm and fish almost untouched by the war. In order for them to get there, they had to cross the major Onitsha-Enugu road which was now the red line and a battlefield riddled with landmines near enemy-occupied territory. It had become a danger zone where the adventurous could get caught in a crossfire between the warring sides.

Many times, the Biafran soldiers would safely escort civilians across the red line, and on one of these trips, Precious was asked to accompany her sisters. It was a terrifying ordeal, the sound of gunshots raging in the distance as they ran, bent over to avoid any stray bullets. Although she was under 10 years old, she was able to carry almost as much food as her sisters back to her family.

Ceasefire came in early 1970. The family returned to find that the occupying forces were gone and their house was pockmarked with bullet holes. Precious accompanied her aunt to her home which was near to the location where the Nigerian armies had camped, and they were both shocked at what they saw. Total destruction. There was not a single building standing. Everything had been flattened by rockets and bombs.

Across the red line was the Nigerian army. Some of the returning villagers would go across to beg for food, but the former enemy soldiers were only interested in the young ladies. Many times, Precious and other children would sit near where food was being cooked for the Nigerian soldiers, silently hoping for some handouts. Sometimes they were lucky, and would get some, and sometimes they would leave empty handed. After the war, some of these young ladies were taken to live with the Nigerian soldiers, and many never returned to Ogidi as they got married to some of the Nigerian soldiers who were mainly Hausas and Yorubas.

Among the many boys who were drafted into the army, were Precious' only brother. Some of her cousins returned safely, but several others, including her uncle's only son, did not make it back from the war. Nobody knew when and where he was killed. There was no one who was not affected by the devastation of war. Heart rending cries could be heard all across the village as they mourned those who were lost to the war.

Precious' brother who was wounded during the war returned home with their uncle, an army general. Her mum and the entire family were overjoyed to see him back safe and sound.

The effect of the civil war is still impacting the lives of many Igbos today. War at all cost should be avoided. Civilians are the ones that suffer the most from the devastation and destruction left behind.

CHAPTER 4

REBUILDING AFTER THE CIVIL WAR

The family gradually began to rebuild their lives. Precious' grandfather who left with them, died during the war, and did not return with the rest of the family. After the family settled back in, they conducted funeral ceremonies for the people who did not make it back.

Sitting down to pick through the debris was hard. Precious and indeed, everyone who had survived the brutality of war, ached in so many places, mourning the loss of so much. Villages had been razed; her grandmother's place was destroyed, her grandfather gone. For a ten year old, this was a lot to process. The tally of losses included some of her cousins who did not return, they were in the Biafran army, and were killed during the war.

New days brought new things. Precious' parents

though pagans, allowed their children to be taken to church by some Christian neighbours, and she was finally baptised. The Anglican Church, which she attended, had specific days when they baptised children from pagan families, and used the day in preparing and explaining the contents of Christianity to them. Subsequently, the young survivor had her first opportunity to attend Sunday school and learn about God; so she grew in the fear of God.

One day in Sunday school, she met her very good friend, Gladys. The war had separated them, and they had all fled to different villages during the war. There was so much excitement as the two girls hugged and laughed, overwhelmed with seeing each other again.

After the war, with life gradually returning to normal, primary school resumed for Precious and several Biafran children. She had been a brilliant pupil before the war, always ranking first throughout her primary education, but her mother could no longer pay her school fees. Since her father, Okoro Nnadi did not believe in girls having an education, it had always been her mother paying the fees from savings out of her housekeeping allowance. Every now and then, when she had saved enough, she would call Precious to her room, open her little tin box, bring out some rolled up notes and place them firmly in the young girl's hands.

"Here, take this for your school fees my daughter," and Precious would hide the money in her skirt and scurry off to school to pay her pending fees.

Sometimes, there would be no money to pay her fees, and she would be sent out of the class which the head teacher found very difficult because of how brilliant she was in school. To manage the situation, the head teacher approached her parents and asked if it would be possible for him to take Precious to live in his home, so that he could put her through school. Her parents gave a vehement "No!" answer. They didn't want their child to become a "boi boi" or, housemaid in somebody's house. Also it didn't make sense, because Precious and her family lived behind the school, just a five-minute walk away, while the head teacher lived in a nearby village that would take her over an hour's walk to come to school. Nevertheless, God was on the young girl's side and made a way for her to continue attending school and classes. It was decided that whenever the staff from the board of education had to come for inspection, she would be excused from school, and after the inspection, they would bring her back. This arrangement continued throughout her primary education.

Like many children of her age Precious loved to play, and it happened that one day she and her friends were playing a catch game, where one child would fall backwards forcefully into the waiting arms of the other children. On this occasion, it was Precious' turn to be caught. As they sang and clapped, for some strange reason, either the other girls misjudged the timing or were distracted, but as she threw herself backward with all the force she could muster, there were no waiting arms to catch her. Instead, she landed on the ground with a severe thud, and her arm hit a large nearby rock. It was indeed the grace of God that it wasn't her head. She broke her wrist and had to be taken to a native bone setter. She was left with a permanent scar on her wrist, and her mother would always admonish her to be careful whenever she went off to play, reminding her of how she got the scar.

As if the scar was not bad enough, one afternoon, in her mother's kitchen, she had an argument with her junior sister, Ndidi, who angrily pushed her. In a flash, being quite skinny and light, she fell toward the burning wood. Trying to break her fall, she screamed and shot up from the floor. The same hand got burnt. But life went on.

Precious was everyone's favourite. Mama Ikenna, her father's elder sister, lived in Ire village, with three grown up sons and no daughters. She talked Precious' parents into letting her come to live with them. By this time, Precious was in primary five. She liked the idea of living away from home because there would be no one to fight over the bottom pot of soup with. There was a particular point when she was quite ill and her parents thought she was going to die. They treated her through traditional means, this was because there was no money, and also due to the fact that her parents believed in native treatment since they were pagans. Luckily, she survived and continued with her education up to primary six.

Nduka, impressed with her results, promised to put Precious through school, and encouraged her to take the WAEC (West African Education Certificate) exams. Precious sat for the WAEC exams and passed, by this time she was 17 years of age. She was also growing into a beautiful young woman and had started having her menstrual period by the age of twelve. She was one of the brilliant students picked for school march-past during the independence day schools events.

Growing up as a child in a very poor family and under challenging circumstances may have been difficult, however the words on Psalm 23:4 was real in her life, *"Even though I walk through the darkest valley, I will fear no evil, for you are with me; your rod and your staff, they comfort me."*

CHAPTER 5
TEENAGE LIFE EXPERIENCE

With growing adolescence, came feelings of attraction to men, but she remained very reserved. Some of the young boys in the village who were trying to date her became nasty when she refused, and started bullying her instead. She even found herself the subject of a masquerade song composed by a boy whose advances she had refused. It became common practise that whenever the masquerade sighted Precious, he would begin his dirge about a heartbreaker.

It was all getting too intense for Precious as she was finding it difficult to enjoy herself during any festive period while she was staying at her aunt's place. Such incidents battered her self-confidence as she could not talk with anyone. As a result, she decided to leave her aunt's village and return to her father's house, by then she had completed her primary six and was waiting for her secondary school entrance result.

Precious was about seventeen years of age when she entered secondary school and gained admission in another town called Abagana. This would be the first time she would be leaving home to be independent. It was a big step for her as for any young lady, but she was looking forward to having her freedom. Her brother managed to buy the key essentials for her stay at the Abagana Girls' Secondary School, in Njikoka local government area. He paid her fees, and the school provided a bed and a mattress. He was able to buy her a small cupboard and a metal trunk box to carry her few clothes, after which there was no money left to buy books or provisions. She was then able to buy one packet of cabin biscuits, soap and chewing sticks. They did not use toothpaste back then.

School life was new and challenging. She arrived with girls in her year to meet senior students who were there ahead of the new entrants. The incoming junior students – Precious and her mates - were distributed among these seniors to be their school daughters; an euphemism for serving them. Part of this role included fetching water, washing clothes for them, and generally acting as apprentices to these big girls. She was deeply saddened by the fact that at the beginning of every school term, her school locker was always bare; maybe just a packet of biscuits and two tins of sardines, and that would be all. She found herself depending more on school food, but she concentrated on her studies, still.

Throughout her secondary school days, Precious was always in class A, which was where brilliant students were placed. There were other bright students in the school, unlike in her primary school days; but she was always among the first ten. In her third year, a female teacher, Miss Madu liked her so much that Precious virtually moved in to the staff quarters with her. She cooked and cleaned for her, and was not sleeping in the school dormitory anymore. Some of her friends were not happy about it because it meant that she no longer had time for them. That year for the first time, her grades went down. She dropped to the first twenty from being in the first ten. When she returned the following year, she gradually pulled away from the teacher, and started staying more in the dormitory to study. Although she still helped the woman from time to time, she minimized the number of times she stayed in the staff quarters where she had little time to study.

Eventually when she was in her fourth year, she was encouraged to go and take the GCE exams and she got an "A" in Maths; three additional A-Cs in Maths and other core subjects in her WAEC exams. Precious ran the 400metres, 100metres, 200metres and the relay race. Her school team went for competitions in different schools and she was always on the team. She was also an active member of her school's debating society. On one of their debating trips, the topic was on bride price and she was the team leader. They won, but during another outing to a radio station, her school came second place.

Amidst all the activity, she had transformed to a

beautiful teenager who was attracting more suitors. Some of her friends wanted their cousins, or their brothers to be her boyfriend, but she was very choosy. She started to do what other young girls did. Whenever she travelled home on her way back to school, she would hitch a lift back; but she was still a reserved girl, and was not flirting with those men. After they had dropped her off, she would always give them a wrong name so she wouldn't see them again. Since there were no mobile phones you could only go to the school in person if you wanted to see someone.

One particular boy, Zik, who was from a boy's school in another town was very interested in her, but Precious already had a boyfriend in her village. One day, both boys came to her school's inter-school sports. The struggle was on to make sure that the two did not meet. In the process, Zik got angry and left, and later in the day, Precious learnt that he had an accident. She felt very bad. His friend tried to rally him and other friends to beat her up in the nearby market close to Zik's school, but fortunately for her, by the time she got to where they had laid ambush, they had already left. So Precious never saw him again, but felt guilty that she did not at least write to him to apologize for not reaching out after his accident. After that episode, she decided to cut off from all her admirers and keep only Jimmy, the first boyfriend she had in the village.

After her GCE exams in 1980, she returned to the village. One afternoon, she, Jimmy, her best friend Ngozi and Ngozi's sister, Ebere were going to visit her aunt in another village. As they were walking, Precious noticed that Jimmy was walking behind and spending more time talking with her best friend, Ngozi, than with herself. She did not like it, because she couldn't understand why the two of them would withdraw from the rest and would talk to only each other till they arrived at their destination. From then on the relationship went sour. With mutual suspicion, the relationship eventually broke up, and Precious travelled to the city to be with her aunt from her maternal side.

In the city, Precious began to look for a job, but everyone her aunt introduced to help her find a job wanted her to be their girlfriend. It did not matter with these men whether they had families, they were still looking for young girls to sleep with before they would help. Precious, being a reserved girl, refused and unfortunately the jobs refused to come. Eventually one of her girlfriends whom she met in the same city informed her of a vacancy in a printing press that was owned by her fiancée. He invited them to come and work for him temporarily for a few weeks. Although it was only for a couple of weeks, Precious accepted the job gladly. Some years later, her friend eventually married the owner.

CHAPTER 6

MARRIAGE PROPOSAL

Precious began dating her boyfriend Jimmy. When the relationship broke up, she started dating another young man who lived in the same compound, although she knew it was not going to lead to marriage. One day he came back with a woman from his village whom he had married. That was the end of their relationship. After that, Precious had two other brief relationships before she finally met her husband. One was with her landlady's son, Kay, who had fallen in love with her and wanted to marry her. They courted for six months before he left for his Youth Service in another state. It was through him that Precious eventually met her husband, James.

One Christmas season while she was dating the landlady's son, as they were all from the same village, they went home together. One evening, Kay came to visit Precious with his sister and cousin, James who had just arrived from overseas. Precious found James quite talkative and wasn't impressed at first. The young men finally left, greeting her parents on their way out.

Early the following morning, one of Precious' distant aunties arrived. She took Precious aside and asked her, "Who were the people who came to your house the other day, Precious?"
Precious replied that they were the people she lived with in the city. Her aunt reminded her that they had come with someone else. She asked Precious if she liked the man who they said was their cousin. She was surprised. She saw him there for the first time, and she told her aunt so. Her aunt said, "Oh, that is the man I told you about, that when you finish school one of my cousins is going to marry you."

Her aunt was not the only one. Upon her finishing secondary school, she was now seen as being of marriageable age so many of the women around her came on behalf of potential suitors. Some of them were Catholics, which Precious didn't want because she was Anglican. At that point, she did not tell her family that she was dating the proposed suitor's cousin. Her aunt went to Nkwelle village to speak with James, and the next day, he and his cousin came to see Precious again.

Later that evening, James thought about his visit. Such a coincidence. He had no idea that Precious was the woman he had been told about previously, and thought he had gone to her house with his cousin for just a friendly visit. He whistled in amazement. He remembered how his aunt had pulled him aside and told him excitedly, "The place you went to was the home of the lady I was talking to you about." He still remembered how surprised he was when he found out that his cousin was not only interested in her, but was also dating her. Something had to be done about this as things were now unraveling so fast.

Precious, on her part, was in disbelief. How could her boyfriend's cousin also want her hand in marriage? She asked herself. Things were getting complicated, and Precious knew that keeping the relationship with her boyfriend a secret from her parents was no longer possible therefore she had to do something quickly. She then summoned up courage to tell her parents about her boyfriend, and to her disappointment they objected immediately, stating different reasons why they would not allow her to get married to Kay. Precious was devastated, but her aunt whom she was living with kept encouraging her that God knew best. Precious knew that she was fighting a losing battle because in her culture, the parents will have the final say of whom she should marry and not the other way round.

Feeling quite upset and confused, she asked the advice of her male cousins whom she had much admiration and respect for, and they all told her to marry James since her parents had rejected her Kay. Precious hadn't made up her mind, until she went with one of her cousins to see her boyfriend. He told her that he loved his aunt so much that he would not want to upset her. Besides, James was his first cousin, and all his family members wanted him to be the one to marry her. He then declared that he was stepping aside because he did not want to cause any problems in his family since her aunt had already told Precious' parents about

James long before he started dating her. Precious was hurt that he could not even put up a little fight to ensure that she was his, and wondered, if it had really been true love. Why would he decide to step aside so quickly? However Precious did not tell him anything about her parents' objections to their marriage. As far as she was concerned, he was the person she knew and wanted to marry, but the young man had made up his mind and bowed out to give his first cousin, James, the opportunity to marry her.

After the Christmas celebrations, and just before the New Year, Precious had to go back to the city straightaway because of an interview she had coming up. On getting to the city, she contacted the person who had called her for the interview, and the man came, picked her, and said he was taking her to where the interview was holding. He took her to a hotel. He was the same man her aunt had begged to find Precious a job. Turning to Precious, he said, "This is the room where we are going to conduct the interview." She came in only to see a bed and one table. She sat on the chair near the table and he offered her snacks before the "interview." Precious was very disappointed, she got up angrily, opened the door, and left. That was the end of the interview and the job never came and Precious went back home.

It was Boxing Day and the village was bustling with activities, everyone was looking forward to celebrating the New Year in a few days' time and Precious went out with her cousins to visit her boyfriend and his family. James came alone the following day to see her, and they spoke for a long time. Precious asked him if he knew she was going out with his cousin. He stated that he knew, and there wasn't any problem with that since they had not been dating that long. So, that was how at the age of twenty one going on twenty two, James informed Precious of his intention to make her his wife if she will accept him. Precious did not agree straightaway and needed a few days to pray about the situation. Some days later, she had a dream where she saw both Kay and James coming towards her, as she started to run towards Kay, she heard a voice that said to her "No, he is not your husband, James is." She woke up from sleep puzzled by the dream. She shared it with a friend who told her that she should see it as a confirmation from God that James was her husband.

Precious then met with James later and agreed to his proposal and shortly after, James went back to his job overseas, while Precious continued to stay in the city with her aunt, and they began exchanging letters.

A few months after they started writing to each other, he arrived unexpectedly. In those days, there were no mobile phones to notify her he was coming. He arrived one evening just before Easter. It was during that period that they affirmed their commitment to get married. He took Precious and his little female cousin who was living in the same compound with her out to a restaurant. They came back that night and chatted for a long time. Obviously, they had a wonderful discussion which ended in him telling Precious they would go to the village the following day to see her parents and tell them he had returned to marry her.

Marriage Proposal

A few days later, they went to the village to meet Precious' family, and it was also the first time Precious was meeting his own family. From there, the process of asking for her hand in marriage began. Before he travelled, he brought his uncles to meet her parents. James went back to his job after two weeks and his uncles started to arrange the traditional marriage rights with Precious' parents. They officially got married nearly a year after they first met. The traditional marriage rights were fully performed with James present at the event and they were together for a week before he put together travel documents to take her abroad.

In hind sight, Precious believed that her meeting with James was all part of God's plan for her life and no matter the circumstances, God's purpose and plan must be fulfilled in her life.

CHAPTER 7
LIFE OVERSEAS

Precious was filled with both excitement and apprehension, the thought of living overseas weighed on her mind taking into consideration that she had never left the city where she lived with her aunt, and couldn't really call herself a city girl because she had been there for only a few months. The farthest she had ever gone outside her village was Onitsha, Enugu and Aba which were still quite close compared to Lagos where she would be travelling with James. What would it be like? What would she eat? She wondered. When it came to food, she could be fussy. She disliked vegetables and many other traditional foods. Salads were not common then as it was regarded as white and rich people's food and Precious was not used to it. When she was growing up, her mother would try to force her to eat her greens, but she would rather not eat at all than eat them.

It happened that Precious' cousin, Nnenna was

also getting married and was about to join her husband in the USA. She would tell stories of how people that lived overseas liked to eat vegetables and would say to Precious, "You better learn how to eat salad because that's the type of food they have over there." Nnenna would always advice, "There will be nobody to make you pounded yam and bitter leaf soup, or okro or oha soup, and you will still end up eating white people's food." Precious would try to nibble on the greens, but it was a slow and challenging process.

She was adapting to several changes within a short period of time and was just twenty three years old when she got married, not fully prepared for married life. It was something she looked forward to although not knowing what to expect in their one year distance relationship courtship. She had never experienced how to handle in-laws and "out-laws" especially. Her husband was a young man, and being the youngest in his family, his older siblings would often make decisions for them and James would always put up with their interference. It was quite a transition and she grew up in a good home where one couldn't exchange words with the elders. You didn't argue with them, and you accepted whatever they said. Being brought up to respect and honor people, this was proving to be a serious challenge.

Precious would discuss with James in private, and since it was his family making the decisions, he would relay to them everything Precious had said to him. She was completely taken aback the first time she overheard him telling his family, "My wife said I should tell you…" She was very embarrassed and had wished the ground could open up so that she could hide. She never expected that he would relay their private discussion verbatim in front of his brothers and sisters who were the deciders of what they should or should not do.

Shortly after the marriage, James insisted on travelling overseas with his new wife. His family didn't think it was a good idea especially his elder sister, Mavis who kicked against it, giving flimsy reasons why Precious shouldn't go with her husband. But then James' uncle waded into the argument, siding with James and supporting the idea that it was only right for the wife to accompany her husband to begin their married life together, since he didn't live in the country.

With everything now settled, excited Precious followed her husband to Lagos where they were to process her travel documents and then catch their flight to United Arab Emirates. Precious was happy when they eventually left his people behind to travel overseas.

Culture Change

She had never been to a big city like Lagos. It was bustling with people and cars, and Precious stared wide eyed at the bright lights and flashy buildings. Everything was so lively and different from Enugu or Onitsha that she knew very well. In one of the buildings, she was surprised as a door opened and they entered into a very small room, with no chairs or windows. She was even more puzzled as some people joined them in the small room. As the doors closed, the room seemed to be moving, she looked at James, and he smiled reassuringly "It's a lift, it will take us to the top floor where we need to go." Her plane journey out of the country, like the lift experience, was also her first time of being on an airplane. Precious had a window seat and pressed her face against the window wanting to see everything. She watched the buildings grow smaller and smaller, and the city lights flickering in the distance like fire flies. It was an exciting time, seeing so many things for the first time.

Precious' face changed in disgust as the meals were served. "What kind of food is this?" She queried. James tried to persuade her to eat some of the mashed potatoes and green beans served with chicken fillet, but she wouldn't have any of it. It reminded her of small baby food. She voiced it out to James who roared with laughter. She watched her husband eat both her food and his. How could he be enjoying this? She wondered in amazement. She hoped when they arrived at their destination in the morning things might be better.

On arrival, they checked into a hotel where they would stay for a couple of days before they made their way to the ship where James worked.
It was also her first time at sea and the challenges she faced were many. Getting into a big city like Lagos for the first time, getting into a plane to travel for several hours then landing in another country filled her with both apprehension and excitement. She was in a strange land, with strange people, but

she was happy to rely on her husband James.

Her first meal was breakfast which consisted of bread, toast and egg. It wasn't too bad, she thought. Dinner was a buffet with many options to choose from. Precious wandered round and couldn't find anything to eat. There was rice but there wasn't any Chicken or Beef stew like back home. There was only curry. She didn't know what curry was and didn't like the look or smell of it.

The meat was not cooked. There was raw meat on a skewer and you had to grill it on the lamps they had on the tables. As a fussy eater, she was facing a nightmare with the change of diet. That night she didn't eat. She only ate biscuits and bread.

Later that evening, James gave her a postcard to inform her family that they had arrived safely. That was when trouble started. In the postcard, Precious wrote that her biggest problem was food, because she couldn't eat what they had. After reading the postcard, her husband became furious. "So, you want to tell your family that I brought you out here to starve you?" That was their first quarrel and he became violent, but when the dust settled, he was begging for forgiveness.

Before she got married, Precious had vowed that she would never allow any man to abuse her physically, and if any man laid his hand on her, she would leave. Yet her husband had just given her a dirty slap for saying she didn't understand why he was getting agitated for nothing. Eventually husband and wife made up, but the incident left a mark in her mind. Alarm bells went off, what sort of man had she married? How could he flare up for a minor issue as what was written on a postcard?

The time came for them to continue their journey by sea. Precious didn't know what a ship looked like, and she was terrified of this huge vessel in the sea. It was bigger than a house. The banister of the stairs was a rope which she held tightly to as she climbed the steps. She could see the sea waters lapping gently on the side of the ship and she was so scared that she couldn't swim, and kept praying that she wouldn't miss her step. Getting on board was such an ordeal, but she made it. It was the beginning of another journey and another story.

Building a life relationship is a big process which requires a clear commitment before one finally leaps into a marriage with someone they do not know very well.

CHAPTER 8
THE HONEYMOON ADVENTURE

As her husband worked with a shipping company, their honeymoon was on the ship, and it took them to different parts of the world. They sailed to Japan and Argentina. This was during the Falklands War, so they had to cross over to Japan from the United Arab Emirates.

Her adventure continued on the ship. This colossal place on the sea would be where they would live for the next couple of months. There were times when the sea was choppy, and the ship would heave up and down. Precious felt sick and terrified because she had never learned how to swim. James continued encouraging her, "Nothing will happen," but Precious couldn't help thinking that one day she would go to sleep and wake up at the bottom of the sea. Sometimes, the other sailors' wives who were more experienced in such voyages, would also reassure her. Her biggest challenge still was the food and the language barrier. Although Precious could speak English very well, it was her first time having to communicate with people from other countries such as England, Yugoslavia, Scottish, Arabs and Indians. All this was happening at the same time but thank God that James was there to support and helped her understand what was being said. At times, Precious would use her infectious smile to cover up as if she was understanding the accent of the person she was speaking with. She was smart and it did not take her long to pick up and join in the conversations. The cooks on board the ship were Indians, and they cooked the exotic dishes of their homeland. She had never eaten curry nor lobsters before, and had expected to see chicken and beef. Sometimes, they would serve some oxtail, but everything else was strange to her. She wasn't coping well at all.

This created a bit of friction between her and her husband. Her refusal to eat caused her to lose a lot of weight considering she was very tiny to begin with. She was not eating and was becoming a shadow of herself. James was very concerned, but unfortunately, they were in the middle of nowhere with no way to get anything else for her. Even the captain was concerned, that he gave an order for her to go to the kitchen and choose anything she would like to eat, and the chef would prepare it for her. Precious went to the kitchen and looked for eggs and sardines. Funny enough, the sardines did not taste like the ones she was used to back home. She was used to the brand known as Titus, but these ones did not taste anything like it. The first few weeks and months were terrible, but her husband continued to encourage her to try and eat the new foods. Eventually she started forcing herself to eat gradually, trying to think of it as an adventure. In the middle of everything, she became pregnant.

Nigerian parents, being what they were, the first letter she received from home they had asked whether she was pregnant yet, and the constant bombardment of questions put pressure on the newlyweds to start having babies immediately. After they had been on the ship for five months just before her husband's leave, she found out she was pregnant. She was vomiting and had to endure all the discomforts associated with pregnancy along with those caused from being on board the ship. They returned to United Arab Emirates where they travelled to England. It was almost ten hours of travelling.

CHAPTER 9

LIFE IN THE UK

England was disappointing. Precious had a mental picture of what she thought London would look like. She had the idea that the buildings would be more beautiful than anything she had known in her country Nigeria. She had imagined the houses would be made of glass. After all this was where the Queen lived, so it had to be beautiful. On arrival when the Captain announced that they were about to land in London, she looked out of the window and asked her husband, "Is this London?" She was confused because of what she was seeing. They touched down at Gatwick airport. What she was seeing looked like tiny huts from up in the air. She hadn't expected to see bushes either, but there they were along with the tiny huts.

Her husband said, "Oh, this is London, the capital city. We are about to land." The lower the plane got, the higher her disappointment climbed, because her expectations were far from what she was seeing. As the plane landed, and she saw things more clearly on the ground, her disappointment was complete. The drive to North London did nothing to change her mind. She told her husband that they could not stay in this country more than five years. They had to go back to Nigeria.

Shopping for food was a nightmare too. In each supermarket, she would walk from aisle to aisle expecting to see the type of food she was familiar with, but none of them had her type of food. Everything looked strange. She was relieved by one thing, the man they were staying with was her husband's friend from Nigeria and he had some Nigerian food, and also told them they could buy African foodstuff from a place called Finsbury Park.

So here she was in Britain, pregnant on arrival, and because they only had their traditional marriage back home, there was no marriage certificate. They had to quickly organize their church wedding. A friend of her husband helped them to find a church where they began to attend, and the Reverend there agreed to wed them. Quickly, they started making arrangements for the wedding. Obviously, both sides of the family couldn't come, but one of her best friends came all the way from Nigeria.

The wedding was held in London and it was well attended, because Precious' husband, James, had invited the few friends they knew along with people from their home town, Ogidi, who lived in England. Her husband contacted his friend to stand in for her parents and give her away. Coincidentally, she was related to the man who gave her away, but didn't realize this until many years later when her mother visited England and pointed it out to her that the person who gave her away at their wedding was a close cousin of her father. It is indeed a small world.

The wedding went well except for one minor hitch - the video man did not turn up and they didn't get a video recording of this special day. The bride was disappointed that she did not have a video of her wedding, but thankfully the photographer was there to capture the event.

After the wedding, and just before her husband was to return to work, they decided that Precious should move in with her new friend who had a spare room. So Precious went to stay with her, and they looked for a school for the newlywed. Since she was good in Mathematics and Science, Precious' heart desire was to become an accountant. When she tried to register to study accounting, she found that although her Maths grades were excellent, her English results were not as good; this meant she could not get admission to study accounting. So, she opted for catering instead, and did different aspects up to the catering professional certificate.

Six months after arriving in England, she had her first baby. James returned for his leave just before the baby was born, and they had a wonderful celebration for the baby. They were both very happy. During his trip back, they bought a new house which was where the baby was born. Precious was eager to find out all the places he had been on his ship while she was in England. In the process, he mentioned how he went clubbing with some of his colleagues and some girls. Precious pressed further to find out what happened. He began by saying he resisted, and then went on to say he slept with one of the girls. He laughed as he made the revelation. An irritated Precious watched his smug look and unrepentant attitude, being quite furious, she lost it and slapped him. This was unheard of in her culture. Though not a violent person, she felt disrespected. They made up and she forgave him, but his African man's attitude did not stop. All she could do was to build her home the best possible way.

Sometime after that episode, the home phone rang, and a woman requested to speak to James saying she was his girlfriend. Precious had decided not to disturb herself with his philandering, so this time she called him, "Honey! There is a woman who wants to speak to you, and she says she is your girlfriend." James glared at her. "How dare you say such a thing?" Precious replied that it was exactly what the lady had said. Angrily he took the phone, "I don't know who you are!" he shouted down the line. After warning the caller not to call again, he slammed the phone back on the receiver. Almost immediately, the phone rang again. Precious answered, and it was the same woman again. She insisted she had met James in Nigeria during one of his visits. Unperturbed, Precious replied, "No problem, do you want to come to the house? If you want to come, I can give you the address so you can see him." James was listening and was shocked to hear what Precious was saying, so he grabbed the phone again and put it down. Precious had handled it with maturity, and of course, that was the last time the woman called her home again.

At this point Precious had to quickly adapt to the culture in UK as well as take a mature approach towards her relationship with her husband. She knew that she needed to depend on God to help her take care of her young family in a foreign land where she did not have any close relative around.

CHAPTER 10

THE GATHERING STORM OF LIFE

There was a recession and there was deep crisis in the oil sector that resulted in many companies laying off their staff. James was home on leave during that period and was confident his job was secure. Unfortunately it wasn't, he too was laid off unexpectedly.

He was devastated. He hadn't anticipated he would ever lose his job and had no other plan in place. He didn't know how he was going to cater for his new wife and baby. Precious was not working and was still on break from studying, so no second income was coming in from anywhere. All his dreams had been shattered, one of which was to put his wife through school, and when she graduated, she would do the same for him. This was a disaster. What was he going to do? Every plan was now affected and some things needed to be put on hold.

Precious began to notice that James was becoming easily upset and was also physically abusive toward her. He also seemed to resent the baby. On one occasion she had gone to see the doctor, and because in the African culture you don't discuss what you are going through in your marriage, she didn't really want to disclose anything. Eventually, she had to open up to the GP. Later the Doctor called her husband and asked him if he wouldn't mind being referred to see a psychiatrist for an assessment. James was so furious when they arrived home, that he became more violent. The job loss had created an unimaginable turbulence in their marriage and Precious did not know who to turn to as her family were far away.

James decided that he would study some short courses to improve his career prospects in finding another Electrical Engineering job in the main land. He enrolled again in a technical college outside London, but while he was there, there was still the issue of no income. Precious was not working, and was now in school, he had to pay both school fees and the mortgage. At this point depression reared its ugly head quickly.

Eventually, he found another job, but the pay was below half of his previous job. Besides the low pay, he fell out with his colleagues. As an African man, James found the younger white colleagues were disrespecting him even though he was more educated and experienced than they were. After a few months he could no longer take it and was dismissed after a heated argument with one of his colleagues.

With all the pressure he was facing, James had to ask his family for support. He told them how his wife had suggested to visit a doctor to assess his mental health, and they made nasty comments which made him even angrier at Precious. The situation deteriorated. One day as he was returning through Gatwick Airport from his last job in the Middle East he had a big fall out with the taxi driver who picked him, and the angry driver dropped him in the middle of the motorway. Luckily, he managed to get a lift home. When he entered the house he was visibly agitated, and worried. Precious called one of his elder brothers back home and explained what was happening, hoping that as an older person he would be more understanding. She later found out that it was a big mistake. His family then persuaded him to come back to Nigeria. When he got there, they took him to a native (traditional) doctor. It was a terrible experience as they took him to a grave yard to perform certain rituals. When he returned to England, the situation became worse. From that time everything went downhill, it felt like a great storm had been let loose on their marriage, with only brief sunny spells. The periods of stability and happy family life became few and far between. Some of James' friends were envious of how doting they were to each other at the onset of their marriage. Sadly it had only been a passing phase. The issues had now become full blown. In Africa the term "mental health" was like a swear word and unacceptable. As it peaked, so did the violence, and every now and then Precious would seek refuge in the Women's Refuge Home. There were episodes she could not share with anyone. The last time she did, her husband had burst into a fit of rage. Her parents were far away, and they had no phones. All she could do was write letters, and how much could she put down in the letters? She was completely isolated, but was determined to study and get good results to enable her to start working.

By the time she finished her initial studies, she was pregnant with her second child. After having the baby, she worked for a little while before her husband decided he was going to sell their property because the mortgage arrears were increasing, and he didn't want to lose it. When they had decided to sell, a neighbour who had noticed what had been happening over time reached out to Precious. She was an older woman who had lived in the neighbourhood for several years before Precious and James moved in. She had watched James' strange behaviours and suggested a church they could go to for help. It was a local Seventh day Adventist church, and they promised her husband could be cured. That was the beginning of her steps toward helping her husband.

CHAPTER 11

SEARCHING FOR GOD

Growing up, Precious had been close to God, but had taken a back seat when she became a teenager. Although she was happy to be married into a Christian home, she knew her personal relationship with God was far off. To her, going to the Seventh Day Adventist Church was a way of coming back to God and renewing her faith, but her primary purpose for going there was still to get her husband healed. It was during that period that she had her second baby, and they also decided to sell their property.

A member of the congregation, whose husband was a leader in the church, told her husband that Precious and her family were selling their house. By this time the house had appreciated in value, they would then have enough money to return to Nigeria as they had initially planned.

They finally sold the house and moved into a temporary accommodation while awaiting James' final decision. Most of the money was kept in his account. He later changed his mind on them moving back to Nigeria and decided to get an alternative accommodation, so they started house hunting again.

One of the leaders in the church tricked James into giving him a loan, and he gave away most of the money. By the time the house they wanted to buy was available, they didn't have enough money to put down for the deposit. This in turn, meant they had to borrow more money than they intended. When the time to pay back the loan came, the church leader didn't have the money. James was angry and blamed Precious for taking him to the church. He also banned her from going to or associating with anybody from there.

He would be so angry whenever he found out she had been in contact with the church members that he would physically beat her up. Once again Precious was isolated, except for the people who contacted her by phone, and even at that, her husband would monitor her conversations to know what and who she was talking with. If they mentioned his health, he would call them back and verbally abuse them. The loneliness and isolation grew. She was always grieving in her heart, asking God many questions. Why was He allowing this to happen to her? How did her life turn out this way? She was always grieving, but something inside her never gave up. She was even blaming God for allowing her to marry James. For almost a year her husband banned her from attending any church or communicating with anybody, and even banned her from praying or reading her Bible at home.

A few years later they lost their new house because James did not have a steady job, and although Precious had a night job, her pay was not regular either, and she was already juggling with so many things. She was studying, she was working, and she was also looking after the children in addition to managing her husband's unpredicted health changes.

A terrible incident occurred just before they lost

their property. Precious was so physically abused by her husband that the police would be called on some occasions.

On one occasion he got into an altercation with them, and there was a fight. James was arrested and taken to prison for breaking a police mobile radio. According to the police report, his odd behavior in prison made the police request for a mental health assessment.

When he was assessed, they felt he had mental health issues. Instead of putting him in prison for breaking police property, he was placed in the hospital arm of the prison until they could arrange for a transfer to a local hospital. He was officially diagnosed with mental health issues in 1989 after nearly eight years into their marriage and out of those years, 50 percent had been complete turmoil.

Precious had been given a student visa initially, but in the course of studying and taking breaks to have children, she was denied a renewal. She appealed, and even their MPs got involved. The first time the MP got involved, they extended her visa, but it expired again after she had another baby. This time there was an outright refusal, which meant she would be asked to leave the country with her family. To make matters worse, James was no longer working abroad, and he too had been extending his visa. This latest development was a huge challenge, but in every trial, they saw God work for the good of those who love him.

They had now exhausted their last appeal, and Precious was asked to leave. That was when somebody introduced them to another solicitor. (This was before they lost their property). The lawyer said if they had a house, that would help them to remain in the country, so they used that advantage, and eventually they had indefinite right to remain in the UK. Owning a property had helped them with their documentation to get residence in the country and when they lost their property, they relocated to another part of the borough where they lived for some time, before they were re-housed.

Many months after losing their property, they decided to start all over again. Precious had their third child, and they were re-housed. When they got to their new place, James tried working for himself. He was an electrical engineer, and he loved maintenance jobs. He was now working as a contractor in a building maintenance company. For the couple of years he was there, there was stability in the family, however, his health challenges did not go away, and eventually he had a problem at work which stirred it up again.

Precious felt James' family were also instrumental to making the situation worse. She would wonder, could it be because of their social status that they didn't want to admit or associate anybody in their family with mental health? They blamed her, saying it was a marital problem created by her; that she had now become smarter since she was living in England, and had joined those that call the police on their husbands.

Precious tried to explain that it was only when she needed help to get her husband to hospital that the police got involved, but they did not believe her, and rather blamed the marriage; instead of accepting the fact that their family member was ill. This created a lot of tension, and animosity towards Precious whom they felt was the cause of everything.

She carried the burden alone, as her own family could not do much because they were poor. So, there she was, in a foreign country where she knew nobody, battling personal challenges, her husband's ill health, in-laws' poor understanding and verbal abuse, as well as managing three small children all by herself in the middle of a crisis.

Precious was twenty three when she got married, and by this time, she was in her early thirties; still quite young, with no friends or family support. She felt God hated her. She often asked, what she had done for God to allow her to be going through all these challenges. She had thought it was God who told her to marry this man and was not getting any answers, and with that discouragement set in.

Eventually after a year, her husband, James, decided they would go back to the Anglican Church where he was before. Precious being from the same denomination went back with him, and they started to attend services. From time to time James health challenge would flare up, but when it was in remission, they had a good and happy marriage.

It was only when the mental health issues came up that abuse and domestic violence reared their heads, and he would turn against his wife as if she was his worst enemy. Usually, when he was well, he was a loving husband and father, caring much more for his extended family than they actually ever cared for him, his wife and children.

In 1993 after they got their papers, Precious decided they should go home to visit her parents as they had not been home for nearly 8 years. The plan was to travel with her entire family, but unfortunately just few days to their trip, James lost his job again, and decided not to travel anymore. So it was only Precious and the children who travelled.

Precious learnt that life could be so cruel but the process of going through trials was a training ground for the call of God on her life.

CHAPTER 12

THE BREAKING STORM

That year, it was during Christmas that Precious travelled with her three children. Before she arrived, she and James had agreed that she would not stay with anybody in Lagos, though the in-laws lived there. She was to go straight to the village because she only had a three week break from her work. It was a new job, and she was on probation. Upon arriving in Lagos, her brother in-law took them to a hotel straightaway. They stayed overnight, and the following day they travelled to the village. It was a wonderful holiday. The children loved everything they saw – it was their first time of seeing goats, and chickens roaming freely. It was a great experience for them.

Then, the storm struck. Towards the end of their stay, Precious and her husband had an argument on the phone because he was insisting that she had to call him on Christmas day, but then the mobile phones were not yet everywhere in Nigeria, it was either you went to someone's house to call or to the nearest NITEL, the government telecommunication facility; which would be closed for the holidays. There was someone else's house Precious normally went to call, but he too would be on holidays in his village. She tried explaining all this to James, but he wouldn't listen.

On Christmas Day, she didn't have any means of calling him, and by the time she got to a phone a few days later, he wasn't answering her calls. Unknown to her, he had been advised by his brothers to come home and dissolve their marriage. James was to arrive and lure Precious back to Lagos with the children. He came and did as they planned, pretending that nothing was wrong.

Before that, he had already informed Precious' family in a letter delivered by one of his elder brothers, that she should not leave the village until further notice. Her family was worried, especially her parents.

A few days later, before he arrived, and just after

she had received his letter, acting on intuition, Precious quickly wrote to her employer in London to state that she was having some problems back home with her husband's family and would not be resuming on the set date. She added that she would definitely be returning to work, and if for any reason, anyone, including her husband, were to inform them that she was not coming back, they should dismiss the information. She then went to send the letter by courier.

When she returned, she was told her husband had arrived in their village. When she saw him, he was polite and showed no sign that anything was wrong. Precious knew that his health challenge was flaring up again, and was still trying to cover up for him, because that's what Africans normally do. They cover up anything that is wrong; besides, she didn't want to aggravate him. Her parents were constantly asking him if everything was alright. By his actions, they all knew, including her mother that his health was taking a turn for the worse. "Have you taken your medication?" They asked. He replied, "Medication for what?"

The following day, they hired a car and left the village for Lagos. Throughout the journey to Lagos, James was telling the driver everything about their married life. It was a jumble of truth and lies tossed together like spaghetti with vegetables. Her entire family life was poured out to a stranger. Precious felt so ashamed, but she had to swallow that bitter pill. They arrived in Lagos, and had an argument about where they would stay.

Ultimately, they went to his elder sister's place, where his siblings executed their plans. That night, Precious went with her husband to visit his two brothers and their families, and as they were leaving they said they would come over for dinner the following day. None of them gave the slightest indication that something was wrong. They did what they would normally do, which was take him aside for a private discussion.

They arrived the following day, and like a gang up, they began to bombard her verbally, "It is an abomination! How can you call the police on your husband?" She tried explaining again how the police were there to make him go to the hospital to receive treatment for his mental health. They didn't want to know. They said it was outrageous; nothing was wrong with him, and they needed to go back to the village to meet her parents. Precious initially refused to go, saying she had just arrived from the village.

What she didn't know was that it was part of their plan to take the children from her. James' brother-in-law, a man they both respected, and who visited them often in London, sat Precious down and said, "Don't worry. We will look after the children, just go and settle things with your in-laws, and when you come back, you can go with the children. It's only a day's journey." That convinced Precious to return to the village with her husband without realizing their plan was to humiliate her and annul the traditional marriage without allowing her to defend herself. So they went. What was the charge against her? She had no idea. They had said, "We're going to your father's place and we will sort things out there."

When they arrived at Precious' father's house,

Okoro Nnadi offered them a seat, and they replied, "Sorry we have finished with the marriage, and we are leaving." Precious was shocked, and asked about her children. One of them answered, "They are our children and belong to us." She requested for their passports and they replied that they had taken their passports; that she didn't send herself overseas, then they left with her husband.

She was in a daze, it was like a bad dream. Eventually, with the help of one of her cousins, Precious managed to get a new passport, and her employer sent her a courier with all the documentation needed to get a visa. She went back to London exactly three weeks after the incident happened. When she got back to London, she went to her house with the police, picked up her things, and went to stay with a friend. Then she began the legal battle to get her children back.

During that period, Precious' in-laws were writing to the courts, saying that Precious was a prostitute sleeping on the streets of London. They said she was being kept by her boyfriends, and they had taken the children because she was not a good mother. It was a heartbreaking period for Precious. Only the prayers and support she received from friends sustained her.

It took three months before the courts eventually ordered her husband to bring back the children, or else face imprisonment. He returned to England with the children. She reconciled with him because she knew he wasn't himself. She totally forgave her husband, although it took her a while to forgive her in-laws because she felt their lack of understanding, jealousy and greed was what drove them to do what they had done. For her husband, although he was the major actor, she felt he was an innocent victim; manipulated to do what he did.

Precious decided to forgive James and asked him to apologize to her parents and her entire family. James took the hard step, and did as she asked. His brothers refused to accompany him, and in the end, his cousin went with him, and pleaded for forgiveness on his behalf. Precious told her parents that she knew that what her husband had done was abominable, but that she chose to obey God and forgive him as obedience is better than sacrifice. She told them how she had an encounter with God as she returned to the UK.

She recalled one evening when she was so devastated with what was happening to her and her children in the hands of her husband's family who supposedly were a Christian family too. She remembered how she was near her children's school and was crying on the street and wondering what was happening to her children that were seized by her husband's family during their holidays in Nigeria. Then suddenly she heard the Lord speaking to her. Although she was in agony, she was sincerely having an audible discussion with God who told her He deliberately gave her James as her husband for her to take care of, and that she should continue to take care of him no matter the challenges as this would shape her destiny and future. She argued with God that if he loved her, he should not have allowed her to be in this sort of relationship undergoing this kind of pains, but God told her that he knew what was good for her. Precious in the conversation replied, "How can suffering be good for me?" God in a space of minutes took her on a journey on that side road to show her how he had created her and master minded everything in her life and what work she would do for him in future through the training, skills and re-molding she would go through in this trial process.

Now that she knew that God had a hand in it, she was no longer asking why as God reassured her that He would see her through every challenge and it would not consume her but would make her stronger. He asked her to forgive her husband and his family and continue to love him more and take care of him even though at times it was very, very difficult for her especially for the fact that his family members were still oppressing her and making each challenging situation more difficult.

She vividly remembered that encounter as if it was yesterday as it changed her life and perception forever. All her questions to God on why he allowed them to take her children or why she was asked to marry James ended that day. She believed she had an answer from God Who explained to her how He knew all about what she was going through, and how He would use the experience for the work He had called her to do. It would become a testimony for many people, so she was to endure. God assured her He would never give her more than she could carry. Those words strengthened her.

After that encounter, she stopped asking God, "Why me?" She was to care for her husband because she loved God, and the man she was married to. From then onwards, her perspective and her attitude changed, and she started to take care of him with joy. It was physically, emotionally and psychologically exhausting and it was a period of stress, shame and disgrace. She took it as a child of God and continued to care for her husband no matter the situation. She even forgave her in-laws and concluded they did not know what they were doing, and continued to care for them. She cared for her husband until his death more than twenty four years later, after her encounter with God.

This is her testimony of how God saw her through all the trials. Even in the midst of the trials, she became the bread winner of the family. God blessed them with another child, so she had four children who saw her go through all the challenges and yet remained standing and believing in God. She didn't wilt because she knew that God was with her, she knew that God would not give her more than she could carry. She knew that her testimony would come, and she knew that God alone is God.

Precious regularly meditated on these scriptures during her tough times:

2 Corinthians 4:16-18 (NIV), *"Therefore we do not lose heart. Though outwardly we are wasting away, yet inwardly we are being renewed day by day. [17] For our light and momentary troubles are achieving for us an eternal glory that far outweighs them all. [18] So we fix our eyes not on what is seen, but on what is unseen, since what is seen is temporary, but what is unseen is eternal"*

Ephesians 1:17-20 (NIV), *"[17] I keep asking that the*

God of our Lord Jesus Christ, the glorious Father, may give you the Spirit[a] of wisdom and revelation, so that you may know him better. [18] I pray that the eyes of your heart may be enlightened in order that you may know the hope to which he has called you, the riches of his glorious inheritance in his holy people, [19] and his incomparably great power for us who believe. That power is the same as the mighty strength [20] he exerted when he raised Christ from the dead and seated him at his right hand in the heavenly realms."

Romans 8:28 (NIV), *"[28] And we know that in all things God works for the good of those who love him, who[a] have been called according to his purpose."*

The lives of Bible heroes like Abraham's trial, David and Joseph's stories encouraged her to endure and trust in God in the midst of life's trials.

CHAPTER 13

BEYOND CULTURAL AND TRADITIONAL NORMS

When you're of African descent like Precious, you're constantly battling the issue of cultural and traditional norms. Most times when somebody is undergoing challenges it is difficult to talk to outsiders about it. Often, the family would want to deal with things themselves. Any offer from outside is seen as "poke nosing" or "too many cooks" getting involved. Precious' parents were not happy at what was happening to their daughter but they were helpless and blamed James' family for lack of support for what was happening.

An introverted Precious found herself at the mercy of these cultural norms and challenges, which at times isolated her. They lived in a small community, and her partner would gather sympathy by discussing their affairs with everyone. This made some people from the community who did not know their story to turn against Precious without hearing her side of the story. Her culture didn't permit a rebuttal.

It was a culture where elders were not challenged, even if they were wrong, or you were unhappy with their actions. Even if it were merely an older sibling, you couldn't express your displeasure. Bound by fear of her cultural upbringing, she chose not to go against what was seen as the norm. Her challenges weighed her down, but she didn't really have anyone to share it with. If it was discovered that she had shared her ordeal with friends outside her community her husband would become violent towards her, and would verbally abuse those friends.

She tried to be respectful to her husband's nuclear family, and tried to be seen as good by appeasing them any how she could, but that never worked. What else was she to do? She was either constantly trying to keep one person happy, or trying to make another one to like her. She tried to make them understand that she really was a good woman and that she needed their support. Unfortunately, nothing made things better. The more she tried to appease her husband's family, the more she felt oppressed by them.

It was all about control. Each one wanted her to do whatever they said. She did not own herself. She felt trapped, like a butterfly in a cocoon, trying to please everyone and pleasing no one. She came from a poor family, so there was no one to speak for her. Her own family could not do anything, her husband's family felt they were richer and more influential in the society.

She was no longer the perky and articulate maiden of years ago. Her sparkle was gone. She felt her confidence slipping away, and would spend days crying. She had wanted to marry somebody else, but she believed God wanted this one. Why would God say He loved her, but allow this to happen to her? She had no friends. Every friend she had was taken away from her by circumstances. She felt her name was anathema within the community. The same people that were meant to be supporting her now saw her as the villain due to lack of understanding of mental health challenges.

She no longer wanted to leave the house, she became apprehensive, and felt that her personal issues were now public, and everyone would be talking and judging her. She began battling depression, but yet she still had to cope with the day to day challenges at home. There was nowhere to turn. Precious found it challenging waiting on God, waiting for Him to take away this situation, her pains and the hatred from her husband's family.

Her husband's family felt that she was the one who had stopped him from sending them money. It was all about money. Her husband used to send them everything he had before he got married. After he got married, they felt they were losing control, and he was no longer giving them like he used to. To make matters worse, his wife, Precious was now telling them there was a health issue. How dared she suggest such a thing? Their social norms would not allow them to accept that their son was going through a mental breakdown. A stigma was attached to mental health problems in Nigeria. In her community, it was acceptable to say that somebody was going through a breakdown, but to say a *mental* breakdown was seen as "madness." Not so in the western world where the expression mental health is a catch-word that covers anything pertaining to the human mind. In the West, depression falls under mental health, eating disorders are mental health problems; a lot of issues fall under mental health challenges. To marry the two worldviews was virtually impossible. If there was an issue with her husband's mental health, they didn't want to know to what extent, and they didn't want to know what could be done to help him get back to his normal state.

For somebody who was a high flyer with a good job suddenly losing it, how could it not occur to them that this was enough to trigger it? There was no discussion in that direction. Instead, they majored on what she termed as "BSE" - Blame Someone Else. They had to blame Precious, they needed to blame the marriage for any health issue their brother had. They would not even accept that there was any health issue, which actually made the matter worse. When you insist there is no problem, how do you find a solution? There was no support except from a few friends and the church who did all they could to support her from as much as they could. Precious will never forget them as they also shared in her pains. They supported her with prayers, counselling, emotional and financial support.

CHAPTER 14
THROUGH IT ALL -

*When Jesus says yes nobody can say no.
Life is a journey and just as in any journey,
you will come to different junctions and meet
different people and challenges, but the journey
must still go on till the end.*

Precious was so angry about what had happened to her, that she was blaming God for even allowing her to be born. She felt it would have been better for her if she was still back in the village, happy as she was before this exposure which she saw as gigantic leap. Not fully happy, maybe, because she was not close to her father, which was also a concern; but at least she was very close to her mother. She could find solace in Mama and her friends in her village, as well as her other extended family members on both sides who loved her.

Throughout her trials, God strategically brought people to help her, including her employers in a

UK government department. They sent her all the papers she required after she had contacted them informing them of her ordeal. One of her cousins helped her to process her papers and bought her a return ticket to the UK. That was a turning point in Precious' life. She returned to the UK without her children, but she fought to bring them back. She went through the court process with support of many close friends who were there for her and helped her avoid slipping into serious depression. God raised a standard against the wicked hands that wanted to destroy her life.

Heart of Forgiveness

She was missing her children so much, with no way of knowing what was happening to them. Her husband's health was deteriorating, but what his family had done had turned him even more against her. Precious' heart was still reaching out to her husband because she loved him so much, but they were drifting further and further apart. She knew her husband was being manipulated and controlled by his family, and what he was doing was affecting his health badly. He was completely stressed out. He had so many accidents in the process that would have taken his life but God saved him from them all. If Precious had not come back to the country to help him get back to normality, he would have died ages ago. She was able to get support for her husband, to calm him down and get him more settled. Some other person might have been disgusted with her husband and his family, but it was God who gave her the grace not to be bitter with them for what they did to her in Nigeria, instead she found herself full of compassion for him. When she returned, she saw what he was going through, and her only objective was to help him get back on his feet although they were still living separately at that time for some months. As a result of all the love Precious was showering on him, the man broke down because he could not understand why, with all they had done to her, she was still kind to him.

Eventually he was able to get back on his feet, and by then, Precious had won the case to recover her children. Her husband was forced to bring the children back. Initially, his family refused, trying to use them to extort money from him, but because of the court order, they had no choice but to release the children. God was also using other means to fight for Precious; other means that she could not quite comprehend. People were completely against her husband's family because of what they did to her. People who knew what Precious had been doing to support her husband, were appalled at what Precious' husband's family had done. Some were calling, telling them that what they did was an abomination which God alone would judge.

Then came the day she had an encounter with God while crying, "Why me?" on the street. In a very clear and audible manner, she heard the voice of God tell her she was there by God's appointment. And His hand was in whatever had been happening, or would happen to her in the future, and He assured her that He would strengthen her to do his will. She wiped her tears, and went home happier now knowing that God had spoken that He would help her, He would see her through, and she would use her pain for His work.

When God had said that His hand was in it, and she would use every experience for His work, she thought it meant the solution was near. Little did she know it would linger for many more years, and she would still go through more pains, experience more stressful situations, and be rejected several more times. Nonetheless, she held on to God's promises and always renewed her strength whenever she remembered the story of Abraham, David and Joseph.

God began to deal with her mindset. She went back to study for her first degree. She was both working and taking evening classes. But God favoured her at the university, so that instead of the course lasting for six years since it was part-time, the university assessed all her past qualifications and experiences she had acquired in the UK, and gave her some credits that almost halved her time in the university. That was a huge bonus for her and clear hand of God in her life because that meant she would stay fewer years in the university. She put everything into the course. It was Applied Social Science with emphasis on health. She wanted to study the sort of health issues her husband was having and use the challenges she had in her family to help others. At graduation, she did a comparative analysis using her family as an example, and then was able to set up a community support service.

Personal Development

That was the beginning of what God had told her, "You will use your experiences for My work". The charity which she set up for the community was for those who had had similar experiences and families going through challenges.

With all this, God still needed to deal with the hurts she was feeling on the inside. It was like the Dead Sea, built up with no outlet. So as part of her course, she studied counselling. Obviously, anyone doing counselling needs to counsel themselves first. She needed to do her own self-assessment. One day, the Holy Spirit gave her wisdom to draw a heart, then she put all those things that were in her heart like rejection, hatred, isolation, disappointment, abuse, and every ugly thing that was in her heart into the paper heart which she had drawn. After that, the Lord asked her to draw another heart. She drew it, and He said, "Put what you would want to be in that heart." The other one was a sorrowful heart, a broken heart, but He said, "Put what you would want to be in that heart, what you would like to have inside you." So she put joy, acceptance, confidence, boldness, every good thing she could think of. Gladness instead of sorrow, understanding, joy in the midst of setbacks, she put all the good things she would like to have in her heart, and God asked her to tear the heart with all the negative things. He told her as she tears it, she would be tearing off all those things from her heart. So she tore it. She then put the one that God wanted her to have, the good one, in a place where she could always look at it and meditate on it regularly. Miraculously, when she tore the drawing of the heart with all the sorrow, and negative things, it was as if those things were ripped out from her and she no longer felt them.

For someone who was shy, she suddenly began to experience boldness, she felt joy, and began to use that boldness gradually. She depended so much on God, and had a number of scriptures she was meditating on regularly.

Romans 8:35. 2 Corinthians 4:7-9 & 16-18.
2 Corinthians 10:4-5. 2 Corinthians 12:8-10.
Ephesians 1:15-23.   Ephesians 2:10 . Psalm 23.
Psalm 91. Ephesians 6:10-20. Psalm 51.

She was now coming out in the community to represent people. When she walked out, she would be so nervous and would start praying for the Holy Spirit to help her. She surrounded herself with both spiritual mentors and business mentors. At one point, she had five mentors, three spiritual mentors and two business mentors. She was gleaning from these different peoples' experiences to help her in life. That was how she started to build her confidence. There was one business mentor who was totally stripping her down, and she felt so condemned by this person. But one day, she had the boldness to ask why he was always tearing her down? The person said because he could see what was inside of her, the potentials that needed to come out. In that light, Precious began to see that she had made a lot of mistakes in the process of growing in business, both spiritually and physically. When trials came her way, sometimes she became aggressive in her approach, because she was not used to verbalizing her problems.

God began to teach Precious things. She was a loving person who wanted to have many people around her. However, God began to teach her something to help her grow. He used a main road to explain something to her. God told her, "I want you to understand that when you are walking on the road, this is like your life. On a main road there is a beginning and an end. As you are walking, you will reach some junctions. Some may be T-junctions, some may be crossroads and when you come to those junctions, just assume there are shops. There are a lot of people interacting, and many of them will interact with you, and when you finish your business there, some may enter your vehicle to follow you to the next station or to the next junction. It does not mean you are a lesser person when you leave some people behind at that junction. They have finished the work God brought them to do at that point in your life. So you need to move forward.

Heaven knew that often Precious would feel down because she had lost contact with so many people. It made her feel she was a bad person. But God was trying to teach her that in life, you have a destiny and within your destiny, there are destiny helpers who God will bring, to use as a sharpener to sharpen you. They may become the knife that God uses to prune you. They may be a thorn in the flesh when they come, but it will be for a season. After that, the season will pass, and you will move on to the next season.

That began to help Precious to heal from all the wounds, all the rejection and isolation she had experienced. She began to develop boldness knowing that she would come to a junction, and interact with people there. She had a goal, she had a destiny and a destination. She would need to move on, and then, at the next junction she would meet other people. So, that was what happened at every junction in her life of training and testing.

God also began to teach her about life, and about marriage. He told her that marriage was the highest institution on earth which God instituted Himself beginning with Adam and Eve. And because it is an institution, God used an analogy to explain something to her. He said it is like going to a university, He told her that marriage is the only institution where you never stop learning. It is a relationship, and in every relationship, you continue to learn. Relationships are a learning process, whether mother - children relationship, husband and wife relationship, father and daughter or son relationship, it is continuous learning. The same way it is with God. You have to continuously learn. God began to explain to her that it was just like in elementary or nursery school where they teach you how to count. Counting is mathematics, He said. When you get to primary school you learn mathematics at the level of adding one plus one, and when you get to secondary school, it's another level, and university another. Yet, all are still mathematics. In the same way that you go through different subjects in institutions, in the marriage institution, you study various subjects. If you pass mathematics in secondary school, you will still come across mathematics in university or college and you still have to pass it. It's another level. God said that it was the same in relationships. In a relationship, you will pass one level, then go to the next level, and God uses all these to prune and make you acquire the virtues you need for His work.

These were the ways God began to teach Precious about her life trials. He made it clear that in life, no man can say he doesn't have trials whether they are rich or poor. He also used what was happening in the United Kingdom as an illustration. He said, "Look at the Queen, She is the Queen of England yet her home has problems and she has problems with her children." God asked Precious if she could understand the stress they were going through, although they had money, servants and everything they could possibly want. Every human being in this world has problems, but it depends on how they handle them. So Precious began to walk with God. God began to teach her how to handle emotions, how to handle challenges, how to wait in faith for God's promises to materialize. She began to learn things, she began to trust God, and from there God began to give her different assignments. He started with an assignment in her community. He showed her how to reach out and become the voice of the vulnerable, how to reach out and be a person that unites, to ask the church to work in partnership; using John 17. God told her that the churches should be united, because all the churches were working in isolation even in community activities. God began to give her one assignment after another, and Precious was frightened because most of what God was asking her to do was to pioneer things and she didn't know how they would work out; but God said, "Trust in Me and depend on Me, for you cannot do it by yourself."

Precious found her relationship with God getting

closer. She had come a long way from the days of blaming God for everything that had happened in her life, and blaming Him for making her marry the man she was married to. When she understood that God said, "I, God Almighty allowed this because it is a tool I want you to use for My work which I have brought you into this world to do." Her perception changed. She then realized that her heavenly Father loved her so much; that everybody that had caused her pain or cost her anything was a tool God had allowed. They were strategic helpers, whether they were good or bad ones. They were positioned to sharpen and to shape her to the sort of person God wanted her to be. She began to have hope, she began to see everything as God said; and she went through different levels of continuous training. She began to understand the challenges of waiting, in spite of the doubts and discouragements when the promises are yet to be manifested.

Precious learnt that there would be pains when waiting in faith, there would be times of doubt and anxiety, times of isolation, even a time when people would ask, "Where is God in her situation? Didn't she say she served him?" There would be times when people would be defining you through your problems: they would not define you by the attributes God has given you. There were times she wondered why God didn't answer immediately. There would be times she felt God had left her because He was silent. She wondered, why God wasn't answering her? She forgot that as a father, sometimes, when we are asking, God keeps quiet because He wants us to learn patience. Precious needed that study in patience because situations had pushed her from being an introvert to becoming an extrovert; and oppression had also made her to be proactive in defending herself.

One day, the Lord said, "Know when the lion in you needs to be quiet, and when the lion in you needs to roar." So God was using circumstances to train Precious. Precious had become a leader in the community and there were people who thought they could do better than her. She needed the lessons in patience. Gradually Precious had become a leader both in local, national, and international spheres through the different things she started doing. She served as a trustee in different organizations. A lot of things were happening, and in the midst of all that, she still had to be supportive to her husband, helping him back on his feet, although by then he had developed other health issues including diabetes. Through it all, Precious felt God's love strongly. Her four children grew up in the fear of the Lord, because when she felt everything was against her, the only place she could run to was to God.

When she had finally accepted that God was not to be blamed for what was happening to her, and that He loved her so much more than any other human being would ever love her, she handed her children over to Him. God raised them in the United Kingdom, an environment where young black people either have police issues or other social problems, yet God showed her that He was the God who had spoken to her, who she had encountered. He held her children, He groomed them in the fear of Him. Everything God told her about the charity she started proved true. Through all the troubles, financial storms, all the odds, the charity survived because God's hand was in it. Against hope, it survived for twenty one years and still continuing. Precious followed God in unquestioning obedience even when it didn't make sense to people. She would listen and obey.

CHAPTER 15

EPILOGUE

God instructed her to write and share her experience, to let people who were going through similar situations know that through it all, God would fulfill His promises. The journey continued, accompanied by the joy of knowing that God had never failed her. Sadly her husband passed away a few years ago. Even before he passed away, he had come to realize and was so grateful to God for giving him such a caring and loving wife who despite all the storms, all the trials, had stood by him. She refused to give up on him, learned to forgive him without minding the bad actions he had taken against her. She learned to forgive him, and learned to be prayerful to ensure that he did not miss heaven. Precious totally believed that he made it to heaven and this was her joy. If his making it to heaven was the outcome, then her sufferings were not in

Epilogue

vain. After he passed away, her worry was whether he had made it to heaven, but she had another encounter with the Lord, where God showed her that he did, and that gave Precious great joy and peace. All the suffering was worth it. It had not been in vain. The assignment God gave her for her husband had been fulfilled. That joy filled Precious, to know that the first chapter of the first part of her book was complete. She could go ahead to produce that book with joy and say that through it all God Almighty, the God of heaven and earth, the Alpha and Omega, the beginning and the end, the One Who is and Who is to come, the Ancient of days held her through the waters, through the valleys, through the hills, through the thorns, through sand and mud, through plain and valley, and no matter what, brought her out on the other side, filled with joy. That in all things, He saw her and her family through.

She also forgave those who had offended her, including her husband's family. She forgave them, and she continued to show them love although, at times she received the opposite from them; but she made up her mind that they were strategic helpers God wanted to use to continue to shape her. No matter what they threw at her, she knew God would use the situation for His own glory. No matter the junction she came to, she realized it was only for a season. And she would pass through it, knowing that her Heavenly Father would never forsake her or leave her at that junction until she had completed her assignment on earth.

Precious happily continues her assignment on earth, the ministries God had given her, her journeys in Africa and in Europe which would be another book.

Through it all, she could see the training God had given her through her personal life experiences and challenges yielding fruit for the Kingdom of God.

Precious loudly says, "To God alone be all the glory, honour and adoration for taking her through this journey so far!"

www.ingramcontent.com/pod-product-compliance
Lightning Source LLC
Chambersburg PA
CBHW021115080526
44587CB00010B/528